Canada

- a practical immigration guide -

By Ingeborg Nilsen

DEDICATION

I want to dedicate this book to all the other brave women, men and children out there who have crossed country lines for centuries to create a better life for themselves and to enrich their lives. This book is especially dedicated to the people who have been forced to leave their homes in order to escape war, violence and starvation. I hope you find a better place to live – a safe place you can call home.

CONTENTS

1 Introduction

Let us assume, dear reader, that you have made the decision to move from another country to Canada, and that you wish to make your immigration as comfortable, easy, and pain-free as possible. You have given the matter a great deal of thought already, and your initial search for information has brought you to this book. Maybe you have just set the wheel in motion and are just getting started. Maybe you are far along with the process, and are simply looking for advice on how to complete your move in the shortest amount of time. Or maybe you are still contemplating, looking for information to help you finally tackle this all-important decision. Whatever the case, this book will be an invaluable resource to you.

I am a native Norwegian who have tried to put together a useful and relevant book based on my own experiences and research. This book is an all-encompassing resource that will greatly simplify your move to Canada. Its numerous step-by-step how-to guides and practical tips constitute a complete body of advice that will help you through many challenges along the way. I hope this information can help you fulfill the dream of a better life in Canada.

2 Why Canada?

Canada is the globes second-largest country, and offers an endless variety of landscapes. Whether you prefer majestic mountains, coastal villages, wild forests or pulsating cities – Canada has something to offer for everyone. Many people associate Canada with cold winters and vast wilderness, and while this can be true to some degree, Canada is so much more. Where I live in Canada, on Prince Edward Island, there are miles of golden beaches which receive praise from all over the world, including a nomination as one of Canada's natural wonders. I have included several photos in this book to assure you that Canada has indeed something to offer everyone, whether you prefer mile-long pristine beaches, regal mountains or vibrant cities.

Canada is a good country to live in with a high GDP per capita, a good health care system, long life expectancy, freedom of choice and an openness to immigrants that is exceptional. Canada provides a very good educational system and a good quality of life. Canada is known as a country with a broad immigration policy, and this contributes to Canada's ethnic diversity. Approximately 260 000-280 000 persons immigrated to Canada in 2015 and the number for 2016 is expected to increase. Canadians are well known for their generosity and their openness, and they welcome immigrants with open arms.

If you want to work, study, be a caregiver or just travel and explore, there are many possibilities in Canada and I will cover them in detail in this book.

To-do:

- Learn about Canada by using the links below.
- Brainstorm: Make a list of all the immigration possibilities (e.g. study, work, be a care giver) you have by using a brain map
- Explore your options and start applying for jobs. Read chapter 18 about employment and chapter 5 about studying in Canada.
- Keep an open mind, be patient and stay positive.
- Do you know anyone who immigrated to Canada? Contact them to learn from their experiences and find out if this is something for you.
- There are many useful resources on the internet – use them!

Links:

- Immigrate to Canada, by Government of Canada, Immigration and Citizenship (CiC) http://www.cic.gc.ca/english/immigrate/index.asp
- Canada facts by www.canadafacts.org
- Finding work in Canada, by www.move2canada.com
- Travel in Canada – http://travel.gc.ca
- The Top 7 Fastest and Cheapest Ways to Immigrate to Canada at https://www.youtube.com/watch?v=Q_57RkRvzKk

3 The Immigration Process

If you come to Canada to work, I advise you to obtain a work permit before you give notice in your current job and start the moving process. Moving to Canada before you have received a work permit is risky and in a worst case scenario you risk moving without receiving a work permit at all. This is also the legal requirement if you come to Canada to work.

Your Canadian employer should know the legalities surrounding the immigration process, and as part of the work permit application your employer may need (some exceptions apply) an approval from the Canadian Government to hire you. This is called a Labor Market Impact Assessment (LMIA). In other words, the employer needs to prove to the Canadian Government that it is extremely difficult to find a Canadian employee with sufficient credentials for the job, and therefore you are given the job instead. The LMIA will indicate whether the job candidate has a negative, neutral or positive effect on the Canadian job market, and how hiring the job candidate will impact the Canadian economy. If the LMIA is neutral or positive, you can apply for a work permit in cooperation with your employer. Your employer should guide you through the immigration process and as part of a job contract, I advise you to make sure to include a section providing details about the financing of the immigration process.

For the LMIA, the employer needs to pay approximately $1,000 application fee and post the applicant's job for minimum 30 days on three different job posting sites - one of which has to be the Government of Canada Job Bank - to prove that no Canadians are available for the job. There are certain requirements that need to be met for a LMIA, e.g. the employer needs to document their hiring plans and prove that they won't rely on immigrants in the future. The LMIA was introduced to make it more difficult for Canadian employers to use low-skilled and low-paid immigrants instead of hiring Canadians. You should make sure during the job interview that your Canadian employer is familiar with the requirements and know the basics on how to obtain your work permit. This you can achieve by learning about the process yourself and asking your employer a few questions during the job interview. If you realize that your employer doesn't know the legal requirements for hiring a foreigner and show little interest in providing advice and help, I would think twice about working for this employer. After all it is the employer who wants to hire a foreigner and it is therefore partly the employer's responsibility - along with your responsibility - to know what legal requirements the company has to fulfill to be able to do so. I write this because I know how much resources the immigration process requires. You and your employer must be willing and able to give up a lot of time and money to succeed in this process. The happy news is that if you preserve for a few months diligently, it will most likely pay off.

The immigration process can become a very costly process and you have to keep in mind that in addition to the immigration fees, you will have to pay for the move to Canada, extra costs related to housing and transport during the relocation and many other «hidden» costs. I would suggest that an employer should cover CAD 1000 for costs related to the immigration process and an additional 2000 CAD (more if you are a family) related to the moving process. Anything less than this and you would need to cover the cost yourself as this is barely a minimum.

Figure 1. Different options to make the Canadian dream possible

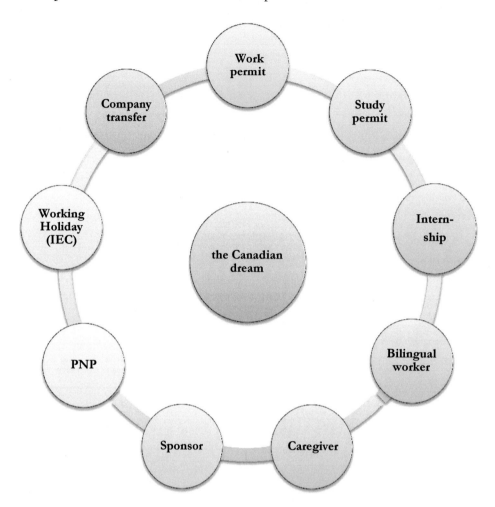

Another option is a provincial or territorial nomination. In the provincial nomination program (PNP), you and your employer have to fill out application forms, which will then be processed by the provincial government. You have to document past work history, family history, where you have lived and traveled during the past 10 years (or since your 18th birthday), your ability to settle in the province (if you have a place to live, job offer, language skills, financial resources etc.) and criminal history. Your employer has to document details pertaining to your job contract and the company, and how the employer will help you integrate into society.

The PNP let provinces choose who they want to nominate and what the requirements criteria are. In other words, they match candidates to the needs of the province. The PNP option is very popular because it gives employers a possibility to circumnavigate the LMIA, so depending on the province it may or it may not be successful for you due to e.g. high competition or lack of attractive skills.

After a provincial nomination is obtained, you will have to get a work permit. This can be done by immigration officers at a land port of entry, meaning you will have to enter Canada from USA by car. You would prefer a land port with 24 h service by The Canada Border Services Agency (CBSA). Many immigrants renew, or get a new, work permit this way so you must be prepared for some waiting. The advantage of crossing a land border is that you can be granted a work permit the same day. I received my work permit this way, and it was a straightforward process. The provincial government was extremely helpful, and the CBSA officer at the border was also very helpful and friendly. A second possibility is to send the application by mail, but this process can take 2-3 months.

If you come to Canada to study, your immigration process may be a lot easier, but the challenge is the financial part of the equation – how will you finance the immigration process, the move, the tuition and the living expenses? Hopefully you can get a scholarship, a student loan or some help from your parents. Chapter 5 «Studying in Canada» will give you more information about this.

Use this eligibility tool to determine which immigration options you may apply to - http://www.cic.gc.ca/ctc-vac/getting-started.asp

Work permit

The easiest route to a work permit for skilled or semi/skilled persons are to get a job offer, and then a LMIA must be passed with neutral or positive result. In some instances there are no requirements for a LMIA. One example is intracompany transfer, where a skilled employee (e.g. executive or manager) is transferred to a subsidiary or branch in Canada. Canada has free trade agreements with several countries that make this possible. Certain job categories (e.g. artists) can work in Canada without a work permit.

If you don't have a job offer, it is possible to apply for an open work permit, i.e. the work permit is not job specific. I would however advise anyone who wish to settle in Canada to obtain a job offer before immigrating.

Another option is a working holiday (international experience Canada, IEC). This is a great option for young people who look for some adventure and useful international work experience.

A work permit permits a person to work in Canada for a specific period of time. The work permit – with exception of the open work permit – allows this person to work for only a specific employer and in a specific position. You can`t study in Canada when you have a work permit, as this allows you only to work. When you receive a work permit, you can receive many of the same benefits as Canadians. You can e.g. apply for a social insurance number which will be valid for the same period as the work permit. You can also apply for a Health Card, which will give you access to provincial health care.

Some requirements must be fulfilled if you are to be granted a work permit:

1. You can only stay in Canada for the period approved for in your work permit
2. You must have no criminal history
3. You must obey the law
4. You mustn't be a national threat
5. You must be in good health

You must be able and willing to provide documentation to verify these requirements if asked to do so, e.g. you may be asked to provide police certificates and a health certificate.

If there are periods you do not work during the time you were granted a work permit, you may have to document this if you want to apply for another work permit later. Documentation could be records of employment, passport stamps, documentation from a doctor etc.

To apply for a work permit, you may have to fill out the following forms:

- Work permit application
- Information about family
- Information about your current marital status
- Information about your use of an immigration lawyer
- Educational and work experience documentation
- A copy of the Labor Market Impact Assessment

The document checklist (IMM 5488,) lists all the different documents you will need for you work permit application. If you follow this checklist, the application process is quite easy.

Remember that you must have educational transcripts, diplomas and other official documents translated if they are in another language. The translations must be notarized by a notary public in the county where the certified translator lives and in some cases also by the Ministry of Foreign Affairs and by the Canadian embassy in the country where you live. Be aware that this is time consuming, so please start this process as soon as possible.

Some occupations do not require a work permit. Examples are students, athletes and military personnel who will be in Canada for a specific time period and for a specific reason other than «regular» work. Check out the links at the end of this chapter to learn more.

You can apply online or by sending hard copy by mail when you apply from outside of Canada. The application process is a little bit different for the two. Since the application and documentation requirements depend on which country you apply from, I advise you to follow the links to learn more about the specific documents you have to fill out. By using the document checklist (IMM 5488) the application process is fairly straight forward.

It is useful to stay updated on the current immigration regulations and laws as they may they change. Many immigration web sites have current updates, but Citizenship and Immigration (CiC) by the Government of Canada has very good news updates and you can subscribe to monthly newsletters.

Document checklist - http://www.cic.gc.ca/english/pdf/kits/forms/IMM5488E.pdf

Processing times for a work permit

Processing times vary greatly depending on which visa office handles your application for a work permit. In Europe, the processing time is one to two months, in Asia and the Pacific the processing time is two to six months and in Africa and the Middle East the processing time varies from two to fourteen months. In addition, I would add one to two months to gather all the necessary documents required for the work permit.

How much does it cost?

The cost of the immigration process varies of course depending on your specific situation, and whether you immigrate as a family.

I can summarize the fees I had to pay to give you an impression of how costly the process is.

- Provincial Nomination, Prince Edward Island 250 $
- Provincial Nominee, Federal Government 550 $
- Work Permit 155 $
- Right of Permanent Resident fee 490 $
- Medical examination 514 $

Total cost = 1959 $

In addition there will of course be a lot of other costs, such as moving expenses and extra costs related to settling down and making a new home.

Moving to Canada as a Caregiver

If you have some experience as a caregiver and is fluent in either English or French, moving to Canada as a caregiver is a viable option. A caregiver can be a nanny, a nurse, a relief worker or anyone who provide some kind of care in a home. Use this document checklist to guide your application process- http://www.cic.gc.ca/english/pdf/kits/forms/imm5282e.pdf

Read more at http://www.cic.gc.ca/english/work/caregiver/index.asp

Express Entry

The new Express Entry system started January 1. 2015, and is a program created to fast track skilled applicants to a permanent residency. A ranking system gives points based on work experience, education, language skills, age and other factors that are likely to make them contribute economically to the Canadian society. Young immigrants are favored, and immigrants nominated through a provincial nomination are also picked first. The express entry track consists of different programs.

If you are a skilled professional (e.g. a manager) the Federal Skilled Worker program is the best option for you within the express entry track. If you have work experience in e.g. manufacturing or processing, the Federal Skilled Trades program is an option for you. The Canadian Experience class is an option for persons who have more than 1 year work experience in Canada. The PNP (see chapter below) is an option I highly recommend as you will get a lot of guidance and support from the provincial/territorial immigration office during the application process.

A labor market impact assessment must be done for a person to be eligible for the Express Entry program. You must also have your credentials assessed and take a language test to be eligible.

Provincial nominee Program (PNP)

Each province (except Quebec) has its own Provincial Nomination Program (PNP). The PNP is a fast-track option to permanent residency, and allows each province to select applicants based on the particular needs of the province.

Each program is a Federal-Provincial partnership between the province represented by Office of Immigration and the Government of Canada, represented by Citizenship and Immigration Canada (CIC).

There are many different "streams" (or categories) in the provincial nominee program through which you can enter Canada. I was nominated in the skilled worker stream (a subcategory of the labor impact category), which demands that certain educational, language skills, work and financial requirements be fulfilled. Other subcategories in the labor impact category are the critical worker stream (e.g. laborers, servants, truck drivers) and the international graduate stream.

I have very good experience with the PNP of Prince Edward Island. I was nominated through this program, and after the nomination I entered Canada at a border crossing, where I received my work permit after a short waiting period the same day. The service and help I got from the Office of Immigration on Prince Edward Island was amazing, and without this help I am not sure how positive my immigration experience would have been.

If you know which province you want to move to, I advise you to learn more about the PNP in this province. This is also an option for foreign students who have studied some years in Canada. To find out if you are eligible for a provincial nomination, it is smart to contact the immigration office in this province.

The immigration process can seem much more complicated when both the provincial or territorial and the federal government are involved in the application process, but actually you will get a lot of assistance and help from the immigration officer in the province/territory. I advise you to try the PNP because if you are nominated, the chance of you obtaining a permanent residency - and later a citizenship - may be much higher.

Compared to the Express Entry track, the route directly from a PNP nomination to a work permit is much faster and much easier. I suggest you try to get a work permit through the PNP in the province you want to live. It took 3 months from I got my job offer until I got my work permit and started in my new job, and I don`t think there are any faster tracks to a work permit.

Processing times

The processing time for a provincial nomination depend on your background and which province you want to live in. Usually the provincial government uses 2-3 months to process an application. When you obtain a provincial nomination, you can cross the land border to Canada and obtain a work permit the same day. If you don`t get a work permit this way (which is unlikely), you can send the work permit application to the federal government (read more in the chapter about work permit).

You must then add the processing times for a work permit. When you obtain a work permit, you can send the permanent residency application. The processing time for permanent residency once you have a provincial nomination varies depending on which visa office it is that handles your application. For most countries the average processing time is one to two years. By now however, you have a work permit, so whether you have to wait one or two years for the permanent residency doesn`t really matter much except for peace of mind.

Links:

- Ontario PNP:
  http://www.ontarioimmigration.ca/en/pnp/index.htm

- British Columbia PNP:
  http://www.welcomebc.ca/Immigrate/About-the-BC-PNP.aspx

- Alberta PNP:
  http://albertacanada.com/opportunity/immigrating/ainp.aspx

- Newfoundland and Labrador PNP:
  http://www.nlpnp.ca/index.html

- Saskatchewan Immigrant Nominee Program (SINP):
  http://www.economy.gov.sk.ca/immigration/sinp

- Manitoba PNP:
  http://www.immigratemanitoba.com/immigrate/

- New Brunswick PNP:
  http://www.welcomenb.ca/content/wel-
  bien/en/immigrating_and_settling/how_to_immigrate/new_brunswick_provincialnomineeprogram
  .html

- Yukon PNP:
  http://www.education.gov.yk.ca/YNP.html

- Prince Edward Island PNP:
  http://www.gov.pe.ca/immigration/index.php3?number=1014385

- Northwest Territories Nominee Program (NTNP):
  http://www.immigratenwt.ca/en/nwt-nominee-program

- Government of Canada, CiC, provincial nominees:
  http://www.cic.gc.ca/english/immigrate/provincial/

Bilingual worker

If you are fluent in both English and French, you could have a big advantage in Canada. Approximately 20 % of Canadians have French as their mother tongue, while approximately 60 % have English as their mother tongue. Both languages are considered official in Canada. This aspect of Canada is important, and the Canadian Government is an attractive employer for bilingual persons.

Links:

- Government of Canada
  http://www.cic.gc.ca/english/hire/francophone.asp

- Bilingual Job Fair Canada
  http://www.bilingualjobfairscanada.com/Default.asp

- Bilingual Jobs
  http://www.bilingualjobs.ca/

- Bilingual Source
  http://bilingualsource.com/

Family sponsorship

Yes, those of you who have a fiancé, husband or wife in Canada are truly lucky. Not only because Canadians are just great. It has to be said that this is one of the more straightforward immigration routes, but be aware that there is a lot of focus on marriage fraud and if you enter Canada this way, you will most likely be followed up by regular visits for a few years. If you have another relative in Canada who is a Canadian citizen or a permanent resident, you can ask if he is willing to sponsor you.

In any case, a person must demonstrate that he is financially able to sponsor you, and through a sponsorship you may be able to move to Canada to live, study or work.

Links:

- CiC, Sponsorship
http://www.cic.gc.ca/english/immigrate/sponsor/index.asp
- Canada Visa, Sponsorship
  http://www.canadavisa.com/canadian-family-sponsorship-visa.html

Internship

Internship is a great way for newly graduated persons or persons with little work experience to gain valuable work experience and at the same time getting international experience and cultural knowledge. There are many different programs for internships in Canada, and you can read more about the requirements and different options by following the links below.

The Federal Internship for Newcomers (FIN) program is one of these programs which let the government and private sector hire interns to fill vacancies.

Links:

- Government of Canada FIN program:
  http://www.cic.gc.ca/english/newcomers/work/fin.asp

- Canadian Careers:
  http://www.canadiancareers.com/internships.html

- Government of Canada, Services for youth:
  http://www.youth.gc.ca/eng/topics/career_planning/internships.shtml

- GoAbroad.com:
  http://www.goabroad.com/intern-abroad/search/canada/internships-abroad-1

Business/investor immigration

You can move to Canada to work as an investor, entrepreneur, self-employed person or as an intra-company transfer. There are various tracks you can chose to enter Canada to do business. If you know which province you will work in, the provincial nomination program (PNP) is a good choice. If not, there are various trade agreements and regulations which determine the requirements depending on what the purpose of the immigrations is and from which country you emigrate.

There are many government funded support programs for business innovation and start-ups in Canada, and in certain provinces the government has developed support targeting certain sectors that are deemed to have a high potential success rate with up to 50 % financing. One example is Innovation PEI (see link below).

Links:

- CiC, Immigration, Business people:
  http://www.cic.gc.ca/english/work/special-business.asp

- Government of Canada, Service Canada, Starting a Business
  http://www.servicecanada.gc.ca/eng/subjects/business/index.shtml

- Atlantic Canada Opportunities Agency
  http://www.acoa-
  apeca.gc.ca/eng/ImLookingFor/ProgramInformation/Pages/ProgramDetails.aspx?ProgramID=2

- Innovation PEI, a support program for businesses on Prince Edward Island
  http://www.innovationpei.com/about

Permanent Resident Card

Your priority when you immigrate to Canada is to get a work permit, study permit or any other temporary permit to stay. Then the application for a Permanent residency follows, which give you the same rights as a citizen except the right to vote. With the permanent resident card, you can stay for a long as you want in Canada. If you stay for 4-6 years, you can apply for a Canadian citizenship. There are some requirements you must fulfill to become a permanent resident.

According to CiC you must have been a resident in Canada for minimum 730 days for the past 5 years, or you must be able to prove that you will be able to fulfill this requirement. Some immigration routes give a fast track to permanent residency, e.g. provincial nomination.

To-do:

- Learn more about the different options that can lead to a work permit and permanent residency – which one is best for your particular situation?

- Do you still feel excited about moving to Canada? Is it a realistic option for you? If so – it is time to get serious. Read on and start making plans.

Links:

- Document checklist for permanent resident application IMM5444E -
  http://www.cic.gc.ca/english/pdf/kits/forms/IMM5444E.pdf
- CiC, information about permanent residency –
  http://www.cic.gc.ca/english/information/applications/guides/5445ETOC.asp#5445E4

4 Employment

I recommend finding a job before you start the immigration process to Canada. This makes it much easier to get a work permit, and your employer will assist you in the immigration process and cover some of the costs.

How easy it is to find a job depends a lot on your skills, education and work experience, and the outlook in your particular field. Retail, public utilities and public administration are among the areas with a good outlook while education, manufacturing and some of the primary industries have a poor outlook. Have a look at the links below to find out more about the Canadian job market. I will also write more about how to find a job or start a business in Canada in my next book.

The NOC (National Occupational Classification) is used to classify the Canadian occupational system. You'll probably have to know the NOC for your particular job if you apply for a work permit in Canada. If you don`t know it, your employer should be able to help you. At the links listed below you can find information about certifications or other requirements that must be fulfilled for a particular occupation.

If you want to work in a regulated occupation in Canada you must have your credentials assessed first. If it is possible for you, I recommend entering the Canadian job market in a non-regulated occupation, as a credential assessment can take several months (in some instances even more than a year). A non-regulated occupation is an occupation or profession where there is no legal requirement for certification. A regulated occupation requires certain licensing by a regulatory body. A regulated occupation is e.g. a medical doctor, a nurse, a pharmacist or a veterinarian.

I will write a little bit about biotech job opportunities in Canada in this book. For other types of jobs I refer to the links at the end of this chapter. I will write more about how to find a job or become an entrepreneur in Canada in my next book.

Links:

- Government of Canada Job Banks, information about regulated occupations: http://www.jobbank.gc.ca/content_pieces-eng.do?cid=202

- Government of Canada, National Occupational Classification http://www5.hrsdc.gc.ca/NOC/English/NOC/2011/Welcome.aspx

Biotech jobs

There are many opportunities in the Biotech industry in Canada as the industry is diverse and because Canada is one of the global leaders in the biotechnology sector. 20 % of Canadian biotech companies have vacancies and a large part of the biotech workforce will retire in the near future.

Canadians are also very welcoming to immigrants, and in some areas of Canada (e.g. Vancouver) approximately 50 % of the biotech workforce consists of immigrants.

Useful web pages (not linked):

- Biology (Career Cornerstone Center) http://www.careercornerstone.org/biology/biology.htm

- BioCareer Pathways (BioTalent Canada)
   https://www.biotalent.ca/en/career-planning

   http://www.biotalent.ca/sites/biotalent/files/PDF/newcomers/BioTalent_Canada_Talent_Opportunities_Nov_13_2013.pdf

- BioScience Careers: Career pathways, career profiles, labour market reports, etc. Registration is required to see all the profiles.
   http://www.utm.utoronto.ca/careers/careers-by-major-biology

- Career Paths (Bio Careers): Career profiles from Animal behaviorist to Zoologist.
   http://biocareers.com/articles/career-paths

- Career in the Biological Sciences (American Institute of Biological Sciences):

http://www.aibs.org/careers/

- Career Profiles (The Scientist) FAQ about careers in biology and industry sectors graduates work in. http://www.the-scientist.com/?articles.list/categoryNo/2916/category/Profile/

Online directories to Life Sciences, Biotechnology, BioPharma and related industries in Canada:

- Montréal InVivo http://www.montreal-invivo.com/repertoires/

- BiopolisQuébec http://bioquebec.com/en/repertoiredelindustrie/

- BIOTECanada http://www.canadianlifesciences.com/ca/db/index.php

- Canadian Industry Database and Portal http://www.contactcanada.com/database/freesearch.php

- Contract Research Map – Montreal http://www.contractresearchmap.com/places/montreal

- Life Science Company Profiles (BioSpace) http://www.biospace.com/company_index.aspx

- Links to CROs (BioPharmGuy) http://biopharmguy.com/links/company-by-location-clinical-research.php

What do Canadians Earn?

Below is an approximate average income by industry. These numbers are reproduced from Statistics Canada (with permission). You can read more about income in Canada at Statistics Canadas web page at http://www.statcan.gc.ca/tables-tableaux/sum-som/l01/cst01/labor93a-eng.htm.

Canadians have quite low wages compared to my Norwegian colleagues, but the cost of living in Canada is also approximately 30 % lower. Depending on where you come from, the wages can be comparable lower or higher, but it is very important that you have some idea about what you can expect when offered a job. Be aware that research indicate that immigrates earn less than Canadians even when they have equal or even better credentials, so learning about the salary level you can expect in your chosen occupation is very important.

Table 3. Weekly Salaries Based on Industry Average

Industry	Gross weekly salary incl. overtime (oct.2015)	Change last Year (%)
Goods producing industries	1,230.68	0.1
Forestry, logging and support	1,117.70	5.8
Mining, quarrying, and oil and gas extraction	1,982.87	-4.0
Utilities	1,824.91	0.3
Construction	1,199.84	-2.9
Manufacturing	1,101.45	4.9
Service producing industries	897.95	2.7
Trade	730.48	2.7
Transportation and warehousing	1,044.98	3.5
Information and cultural industries	1,220.53	3.7
Finance and insurance	1,198.68	5.2
Real estate and rental and leasing	953.36	2.4
Professional, scientific and technical services	1,373.39	4.5

Employee Rights

All employees are protected by different regulations and laws in Canada and employers must ensure a work environment that is fair and free from discrimination.

The provincial or territorial employment legislation protects the rights of approximately 85-95 % of all workers.

Federal labour standards regulate businesses and industry that are regulated by the federal government. These companies are governed by the Canada Labour Code.

Discrimination is prohibited in Canada by the Canadian Human Rights Act (CHRA). Discrimination based on gender, race, ethnicity, age and a number of other grounds is illegal.

The Employment Equity Act (EEA) is another law that protects against discrimination. It protects the rights of women, people with disabilities, Aboriginal people, and visible minorities.

www.work.alberta.ca/workrights is a web page containing information about the provincial and territorial regulation.

The Employment Contract

Never accept an informal job offer sent to you by mail. . Even if a job offer sent by e-mail is - in Canada as in many other countries – legally binding if you accept it, I would still insist on a detailed written job contract which both employer and employee has to sign. If you receive a job offer, take a few days to reflect on it. This is especially important if you need to relocate and move to another country. You must also keep in mind that you must obtain a work permit to work in Canada, so I recommend accepting the job offer pending work permit approval. It is however a given, without a work permit you are not allowed to work in Canada.

Job titles are quite important in Canada, and indicate what compensation package that is included in the job contract. This could be stock options, bonuses, health- and dental insurance and other benefits.

You should be aware of the termination clause in your job contract, as some Canadian employers use the «at will» termination clause. In an "employment at will" type contract, either party may be able to terminate the agreement without liability. If you do not like your new job you can quit your job at any time without facing any serious repercussions. On the downside, however, your employer may be able terminate your job without any particular reason, leaving you without work.

These details should be covered in a written job contract (the employee handbook you will probably be sent separately) signed by both parties)

1. Employee handbook
2. Benefits
3. Relocation expenses
4. Repatriation expenses (if applicable)
5. Vacation and holidays
6. Pension
7. Currency and frequency of payment.
8. Detailed information about employee roles and responsibilities, personal development management and performance appraisal methods.
9. Dispute resolution procedure.
10. Length of the contract period (if temporary job)
11. Qualification that the assignment is conditional upon the employee obtaining the appropriate visa.
12. Tax equalization.
13. Termination of employment, including notice period, severance, repatriation and grounds for cessation.
14. Work hours and overtime pay entitlement.

5 Studying in Canada

Canada is a great choice if you want to study abroad. In fact, as soon as I get my permanent residency I will start a MBA degree in addition to working here. I started a MBA in Norway in January this year, and I could have continued this degree as it is an online education, but I choose to study in Canada instead.

One of the reasons is that the quality of the education in Canada is very high, and with a degree obtained in Canada, your education will receive world-wide recognition. The educational system in Canada is innovative and the focus is on research and practical appliance in the job market. Some provinces are well known for educations that are applicable in the specific province, e.g. Alberta and Saskatchewan are great destinations if you want an education in oil/gas while the east coast of Canada is well regarded in the marine sciences.

The tuition fees in Canada vary, but generally the fees at public educational institutions in Canada are approximately 25-35 % lower compared to USA. Tuition fees per year varies across Canada, from approximately 2000 $ to 7000 $ depending on the province and educational institution. Newfoundland and Labrador is the province with the lowest tuition fees.

Canada is an ethnic diverse country with approximately 250 000 immigrants each year during the last 10 years, and every year approximately 250 000 international students come to Canada. The Canadian Government plans to double this amount, so as a foreign student you will feel welcome in Canada.

Canada can offer something for everyone. The nearest big city is never far, and if you prefer the great outdoors, Canada has more than 40 national parks and can offer some of the world's most beautiful and pristine nature.

English and French are the two official languages in Canada. The majority of Canada's population with French as the mother tongue lives in Quebec. New Brunswick also has many inhabitants with French as their primary language. There are therefore many great opportunities to learn both French and English while studying in Canada.

The Canadian Educational System

In Canada, the educational system consist of diploma and certificate programs, bachelor , master and Ph.D. The French name for a bachelor is baccalaureate.

Colleges and institutes offer also diploma and certificate programs as their primary activity, while some offer degrees in areas of certain specializations. Degree programs may be associate degrees (2 years) or applied degrees (4 years). University diplomas and certificates require usually one or two years of study in a specific field or discipline.

The bachelor degree can be obtained after three to four years depending on the province and the degree. You will choose a major at the bachelor-level, with some additional subjects of your choosing.

The academic year is usually from September to April or May, and consists of two or three semesters. Most academic institutions have admission both in the spring and in the autumn.

To study in Canada you need a study permit. There are a few exceptions, and you can read more about this by following the links at the end of this chapter. To obtain a study permit, you need an acceptance letter from a Designated Learning Institution (DLI): http://www.cic.gc.ca/english/study/study-institutions-list.asp

Time line to get a student permit

After you have received an acceptance letter from a Designated Learning Institution, you can apply for a student permit. Make sure that you have all the other documents that may be required for a student permit in order. These may be e.g. a valid passport, police certificate and birth certificate. Remember that you must have them translated and notarized as described in the chapter "Translation of Documents" if applicable. If you have to order some of them , you can do this while you wait for the acceptance letter.

The processing times for a student permit vary greatly depending on which visa office handles your application. Most European visa offices have processing times from three to seven weeks. In Asia the processing times can be up to 12 weeks. You can read more about the processing times at the CiC web page.

To-do:

1) Find out if you are eligible to study in Canada. You may have to provide a police certificate, a health certificate and proof of financial means. Check out the links below to learn more.
2) Determine which field of study you want to pursue
3) Determine which Canadian educational institutions match you field of study best – make a prioritized list
4) Determine admission criteria for each institution, and the level of cost – make a new prioritized list
5) Apply directly to the institution you would like to attend. Contact the designated learning institution directly.

Links:

- Information about studying in Canada by the Canadian Government:
  http://www.cic.gc.ca/english/study/index.asp

- Document checklist for Study Permit Application (IMM5483)

- A web page by CMEC – the Council of Ministers of Education, Canada – containing a lot of information about the practical aspects of studying in Canada (cost, how to apply for Visa etc.):
  http://studyingincanada.ca/

- Association of Universities and Colleges of Canada:
  http://www.universitystudy.ca/search-programs/

- An interactive web page where you can search for information and create your own dashboard:
  http://www.studyincanada.com/

- The Canadian Information Centre for International Credentials:
  http://www.cicic.ca/857/Study/index.canada

- Education in Canada:
  http://www.educationau-incanada.ca/educationau-incanada/index.aspx?lang=eng

6 Medical exams and police checks

When you apply for a, you may need to provide proof of a medical exam and/or a police check.

Medical exams

When you apply for a temporary or permanent residency you may be required to undergo a medical exam. Sometime after you apply for a permanent residency (for me this period was 3 months), you may receive instructions from CiC to do a medical exam. Only one of the CiC panel doctors can do this exam, and will usually include a general physical examination, chest x-ray and blood sampling. The cost of this exam was in my case 205 $ for the doctors exam and 309 $ for the examinations at the hospital.

Police certificates

As part of your application you may have to provide police certificates from all the countries you have lived. As processing time for police certificate applications can be several weeks, it is recommended that you apply for these as soon as possible and include it in you permanent residency or citizenship application to ensure no undue delays.

In some cases you may also need a police certificate when you apply for a temporary work permit or student permit.

Links:

- Information about medical exams by CiC
  http://www.cic.gc.ca/english/information/medical/index.asp
- Information about police certificates and how to get a police certificate in various countries and territories.
  http://www.cic.gc.ca/english/information/security/index.asp

Reasons that may hinder your immigration process

There are many reasons that could prove it difficult for you to obtain a visa or prevent you from entering Canada. Most reasons are related to health, security and safety, and I advise you to gather information about this before you decide to leave your home country.

A health reason could be that you have a disease that could result in public health or safety concerns.

Security and safety reasons could be that you have committed crimes, belonged to criminal organizations, or have family members that create red flags in your background.

It is also essential that you are forthright and completely honest in your immigration process as giving false information is a crime in itself (misrepresentation).

Every person and situation is however unique and it is the immigration officer who will decide if you can enter Canada when you arrive.

The interview

When you enter Canada, an immigration officer will interview you. It is advisable to be prepared for this interview. The officer will ask you what you are going to do in Canada, where you will stay, for how long you will stay and if you have sufficient capital for this period. You must be prepared to give details and provide documentation to prove what you are saying is true. Be prepared and be honest when your answer.

7 Credentials and Skills Assessment

One of the challenges of moving to another country is that your education, work experience and professional licensing/authorizations may not be regarded as equivalent to the Canadian credentials.

Citizenship and Immigration Canada (CIC) requires that if you apply to certain economic immigration programs, you will need an Educational Credential Assessment (ECA) of educational credentials you received outside of Canada. CIC uses this assessment to validate your foreign educational credentials and to determine how they compare to completed Canadian credentials.

In Canada the job market is divided into regulated and non-regulated occupations. The non-regulated job market is a great place to start when entering the Canadian job market.

You will need to get an ECA for your foreign degree, diploma or certificate if:

1. you want to be considered for the Federal Skilled Worker Program (FSWP) under Express Entry, and
   - you are a principal applicant, and
   - you got your education outside Canada, or

2. you want to receive Comprehensive Ranking System (CRS) points for your foreign education
   - for yourself as an Express Entry candidate, or
   - for your spouse or common-law partner coming with you to Canada.

International Credential Evaluation Services (ICES)

ICES has been designated by Citizenship and Immigration Canada (CIC) to provide Educational Credential Assessment (ECA) reports for Canadian immigration purposes.
Under the guidelines provided by the Citizenship and Immigration Canada (CIC) ICES will only provide ECA reports for completed academic credentials. Note, ICES does not evaluate trade qualifications. For more information about the Federal Skilled Trades Program see this CIC link.
ICES will provide a statement of the general equivalency of international educational credentials to a completed Canadian educational credential.
If you want to work as a medical doctor you must apply to the Medical Council of Canada. If you want to work as a pharmacist, you must apply to the Pharmacy Examining Board of Canada.

International Qualifications Assessment Service (IQAS)

IQAS does not evaluate Trades Training or occupational/professional qualifications and evaluates only formal academic/technical education.
An assessment does not mean that you will get a job in Canada or that you will succeed as an immigrant. It also does not mean that your professional credentials are automatically recognized or will be recognized for licensure in Canada. If you work in a regulated profession, you must still go through the process of getting your license in the province or territory that you plan on settling in.

Language skills

You may be required to demonstrate sufficient English proficiency to apply for a work permit, study permit or permanent residency. Both the IELTS test and the CELPIP-G test are recognized by CiC. The IELTS test is worldwide recognized compared to the CELPIP-G test, which is a Canadian language test. I therefore recommend the IELTS test since you can find a test center in your home country.

IELTS Test
The IELTS (International English Language Testing System) is a language test that Citizenship and Immigration Canada (CIC) recognizes, and you can take this test worldwide.
The IELTS test consists of a listening, reading and academic reading/ writing or general reading/writing test. The academic reading/writing test is for those who wants to study in a country where English is the official language.

CELPIP Test
The Canadian English Language Proficiency Index Program (CELPIP) is developed at the University of British Columbia. There are two different CELPIP tests, and only the CELPIP-G test is recognized by CiC.

Links:
- Designated language testing agencies, CiC:

http://www.cic.gc.ca/english/resources/tools/language/agencies.asp
- IELTS test to live and work in Canada:
  https://www.ielts.org/test_takers_information/ielts_in_can.aspx
- Candidate booklet:
  http://www.ielts.org/pdf/IELTS%20Information-for-Candidates-March%202015.pdf
- IELTS exam
  http://www.ielts-exam.net/practice_tests/

8. Documents you need to enter Canada

Before you enter Canada there are certain documents you need to bring with you in order to enter the country and to obtain the necessary immigration documents. It is the Canada Border Services Agency (CBSA) that manages the import/export and border control in Canada. On their web page you will find more information about bringing goods to and from Canada.

If you arrive by plane, you will be given a Customs Declaration Card. The following items must be declared:

- Alcohol, tobacco and gifts (items that are not duty free)
- Other items to be declared: Plants, food, animals, weapons
- Any amount above 10 000 $

See http://www.cbsa-asfc.gc.ca/publications/forms-formulaires/e311-eng.pdf

If you are bringing any personal belongings with you, another form must be filled out, the "Personal Effects Accounting Document" . As long as you owned and used these items before you entered Canada, you may bring them with you duty free. List all the goods (including value) you bring with you when moving to Canada, including items you will have sent/imported after you arrive. If you don`t include the items on this form, you may have to pay import tax (duty) on them later. Bring with you two copies of this document.

See http://www.cbsa-asfc.gc.ca/publications/forms-formulaires/b4a.pdf

Some documents are essential:

- eTA (electronic Travel Authorization, from March 15. 2016) or visitor Visa (if applicable) and
- Confirmation of Permanent Residence for each family member traveling with you or
- Work permit or Study permit
- Two (2) copies of a "Personal Effects Accounting Document" - a detailed list of all the personal belongings you are bringing with you to Canada.

- Include items you bring with you **and** items that are shipped later, i.e. all personal belongings you bring to Canada

- A valid passport or other travel document for each family member traveling with you

Other documents you may need:

- Birth certificates or baptismal certificates
- Marriage certificates
- Adoption, separation or divorce papers
- School records, diplomas or degrees for each family member
- Professional certificates and licenses
- Employment records (references from previous jobs, tax records)
- A CV describing your educational and professional qualifications and job experience
- Driver's license, including an International Driver's Permit
- A reference from your auto insurance company describing:
  - How long you have owned a car
  - For how many years you have had auto insurance
  - Details about any claims you have had (when, where, at fault or not, amount of claim)
  - If you have had several auto insurance companies, you need a reference from each company
- History of your driving record (e.g. from the issuer of your driver`s license or the police). This will be necessary if you want to buy a car in Canada
- Photocopies of all essential documents, in case the originals get lost (be sure to keep the photocopies in a secure location)
- Car registration documents (if you are importing a car into Canada)
- Medical records (e.g. immunization/vaccination records)
- Dental records

Links:
- Personal Effects Accounting Document: http://www.cbsa-asfc.gc.ca/publications/forms-formulaires/b4a.pdf

- Canada Border Services Agency (CBSA): http://www.cbsa-asfc.gc.ca/menu-eng.html

- Settlement.org, a web page providing information about what you can bring into Canada (and a lot of other useful information):

http://settlement.org/ontario/immigration-citizenship/landing-and-leaving/landing-in-canada/i-am-immigrating-to-canada-how-do-i-bring-my-belongings-with-me/

- CBSA, Information to residents who return to Canada
  http://www.cbsa-asfc.gc.ca/travel-voyage/ifcrc-rpcrc-eng.html

- Canada Post, customs requirements
  https://www.canadapost.ca/tools/pg/manual/PGcustoms-e.asp

Ingeborg Nilsen

9. Translation of Documents

Having your documents translated and verified (by affidavit or notarization) can be a time consuming and costly affair. Make sure you start this process at least 3-4 months before you move. You may also have to visit the Ministry of Foreign Affairs and the Canadian Embassy in your home country as part of the process.

Any document in another language must be translated to English (or French if applicable). The translations must be done by a certified translator, and the translation must be notarized by a notary public, or verified by any other affidavit.

It is not acceptable that documents are translated by family members, neighbors or even noncertified translators.

Links
CiC Translation of documents
http://www.cic.gc.ca/english/resources/tools/cit/admin/general/translation.asp

CiC, What is an affidavit
http://www.cic.gc.ca/english/helpcentre/answer.asp?q=040&t=4

10. Culture Shock!

Your first months in Canada will be full of change. You will face many challenges, especially if you have to learn English or French, or improve your language skills. You may have to take a first job or live in a home that is different from what you expected. You may have to enter the Canadian labor market in a job that less prestigious or pay less than the one you had in your home country. You may need to get more education or training to get an equally good job and to build your new life here. In the beginning you may have problems getting around as it may take some time before you can buy your own car. This is particularly true in rural areas. The bottom line is that everything is probably different from your home country to some degree and his can cause a lot of stress in your life. Common problems include: information overload, language barrier, technology gap, homesickness (cultural), lack of social support, difficulty of navigating a foreign health care and educational systems, feeling trapped as you can only work for a given employer, disappointment in a system that don`t treat your credentials and skills as equal. There is no way of preventing culture shock, and individuals are affected differently by cultural differences. One way to adapt is to take time each day to remember why you are doing this, and take a time out. Do something you enjoy every day.

Some common feeling that may affect you while trying to adapt to a new culture:

- Uncertainty
- Hopelessness
- Anxiety
- Unease

In the beginning you may feel like this is like a holiday. You are fascinated by the new culture and you mostly notice the positive aspects.

As the demands and requirements of adapting to a new country challenge you, and the differences between your home country and the new culture becomes apparent, you may feel disconnected and homesick. Every aspect of your home country appear rose colored, while you may feel unease or anxiety about the country you have moved to.

After several months you may start to adapt to your new country, and you may get a more realistic perspective. Your home country and your new country both have positive and negative aspects, and as you increasingly adapt to your new country you feel more secure and relaxed.

Some tips to make the transition phase smoothly:
- Eat healthy food and get some daily exercise
- Take time out to rest and do something pleasant for yourself every day
- Take the time to explore your new country, be a tourist and create some good memories
- Don`t force yourself to change all your daily habits just because you live in another country. People thrive on routine
- Integrate yourself into the new culture. Make friends and join a club or a gym

Links:

- http://travel.gc.ca/travelling/living-abroad/culture-shock
- https://www.internations.org/magazine/what-is-culture-shock-15332

11. Before and After the Move

Before you consider moving there are many things you will need to consider, some of them are

- How will you finance the stay (work, study etc.?)
- What will you do with your current assets?
- Do you want to use an immigration lawyer?
- Where will you live?
- How will you get around (public transportation or buy a car)?
- Do you have enough capital to manage the transition?
- Do you have all your documents in order?
- Do you need to improve your English or French?
- Do you need to get your credentials assessed?
- Do some career research if you didn`t already get a job
- Do you need to open a bank account in Canada?

During the first few weeks in Canada you should try to get all the essential documents and registrations done in order to start enjoying your new life. Don`t be overwhelmed by everything you have to do. You deal with this as you deal with all other major projects, by tackling one task at a time.

When you apply for e.g. a health card or a driver`s license in Canada, you must present:

- proof of legal presence in Canada and
- primary identification and
- secondary identification

You may also be required to show some other documents, e.g. utility bill or a document from your bank that verify your address.

Proof of Legal Presence and Primary documentation can be e.g.:

- Valid Foreign Passport with appropriate immigration documents
- Permanent Resident Card or Immigration papers
- Study or Work Permit
- Canadian Citizenship Card
- Temporary Resident Permit
- Secure Certificate of Indian Status Card (with photograph)

Primary documentation:

- Government issued Birth Certificate[1]
- Passport
- Driver`s license

[1] if the name on the birth certificate is not your current name, you will require another original of documents such as a marriage certificate which specifies your current name.

Secondary documentation:

- Baptismal Certificate (with church seal)
- Marriage Certificate
- Social Insurance Card
- Credit Card
- Health Card
- or other similar documentation

To-do:

• Apply for Canadian photo identification, such as a driver's license, which you should carry with you at all times. You can read more about getting a driver's license later in this book.

•Find a place to live. You can rent an apartment or house, or buy a property. This is covered in detail later in this book.

[handwritten note:] Can I apply for a Social Insurance Number (SIN) now?

•Apply for a Social Insurance Number (SIN), a nine-digit number that [...] nada to get a job and to pay taxes.

•Get a health card. A health card gives you many benefits, such as cove[...] services, in-hospital health services and much more. See
http://www.servicecanada.gc.ca/eng/subjects/cards/health_card.shtml

•Open a Canadian bank account and apply for a credit card in order to begin to establish your credit history in Canada.

•Get a map of your area and find out about public transportation. You can read more at:

- o http://www.gotransit.com.
- o http://www.cnmag.ca/issue-5/682-life-public-transit-e05

•Contact a school or school board to register your children in school. See
http://www.cic.gc.ca/english/newcomers/after-education.asp

Links:

- • *"Welcome to Canada: What You Should Know"* publication by the Canadian Government:
  http://www.cic.gc.ca/english/resources/publications/welcome/index.asp
- • *Welcome Here: A* website of the Canadian Association of Family Resource Programs (FRP Canada):
  http://www.welcomehere.ca/index.cfm
  http://www.welcomehere.ca/index.cfm?fuseaction=Page.ViewPage&pageId=1092
- • *"Discover Canada: The Rights and Responsibilities of Citizenship"* is used by newcomers to study for the citizenship test:
  http://www.cic.gc.ca/english/resources/publications/discover/index.asp
- • Health card information:
  http://www.servicecanada.gc.ca/eng/subjects/cards/health_card.shtml
- • Social insurance number information:
  http://www.servicecanada.gc.ca/eng/sc/sin/index.shtml?utm_source=Vanity%20URL%20-%20DDN&utm_medium=Offline&utm_term=SIN%20Card%20Termination%20(SCTOP)%2020
  13%2F2014&utm_content=Dec%202013%2C%20Eng&utm_campaign=SIN%20Card%20Termin
  ation%20(SCTOP)
- • Education, elementary:
  http://www.cic.gc.ca/english/newcomers/after-education.asp

The next weeks in Canada

After you have the most important necessities covered, you can start working on the next steps of the settlement process.

The next few weeks you can look into options for internet and cell phone services. Be aware that using the cell phone service you brought with you from your home country can be very expensive and phone bills can break your budget if you are not careful. As soon as you get your immigration papers, you can apply for a social security number. You will also probably need some other form of identification – e.g. a driver`s license – to buy a cell phone and internet subscription.

I recommend buying a phone with a 2-year plan as you can find a deal where you pay only for the subscription and get the phone for free. I bought one of these plans for 50 $ per month and got a Motorola X-Play included in the price. There are many deals and cell phones to choose between, so you will probably find something that satisfy your needs and requirements. See the links below to find deals on cell phone plans. Most large shopping malls have service centers for the main cell phone operators. Remember to bring your documents with you when you go to buy a cell phone.

I would recommend asking neighbors or your landlord for recommendations regarding internet services. I would also recommend getting quotes from different companies as the prices can differ greatly. The internet services in Canada are quite expensive if you want good enough service to stream movies and music. Prices can range from approx. 40-80 $ per month.

To do:

- Improve you language skills if applicable
- Explore your options for telephone or internet service.
- Learn about dental and health care options in your area
- Have your children immunized. Vaccinations are free when you show your provincial health card.
- Apply for the Canada Child Tax Benefit (applicable if you have children under 18)
- Get your education credentials recognized to improve your chances of getting better jobs or to make you eligible for educational programs
-

Links:

Cell phone services

- Bell Mobility shop - www.bell.ca/mobility
- Rogers shop – www.rogers.com
- Telus – www.telus.com

Internett services

- www.eastlink.ca
- www.bell.ca

12. Renting and Temporary Housing

One of your first needs after you arrive in Canada is a temporary place to stay until you can rent or buy a home. One option is to stay at a hotel or hostel.

There are many options to choose between and your budget will maybe determine what`s most practical for you. If you have friends or relatives in Canada, that is a great possibility for temporary housing. There are many web pages where you can search for accommodation. I have listed a few below under "links". In the appendix I have included menu links to immigration web pages, where you can find a lot of useful tips. CiC has created a "Welcome to Canada guide" which includes a lot of useful information.

In most provinces and major cities, there are many organizations that provide assistant to newcomers. I have included many links in the appendix, but you can also find useful information in landing guides - http://www.canadavisa.com/canada-landing-guides.html

If you are a refugee, you will get help finding accommodation through the "Refugees Resettlement Assistance Program" - http://www.cic.gc.ca/english/refugees/canada.asp

Identify Your Needs

Make a list of requirements for your new home, such as

- How many rooms do you need?
- How many bathrooms do you need?
- Public transit nearby

- Distance to pre-school and school?
- Rental cost or mortgage cost – what is your budget range?
- Utilities – what is included in the rent and what do you have to cover yourself?
- Smoking or non-smoking
- Do you have pets – many landlords don`t accept pets
- Garden
- Laundromat
- Parking
- Furnished vs non-furnished
- Are appliances included?

Cost is maybe the most important factor you have to consider. In some provinces there is provincial rent-control. You should check if this applies to the apartment you want to rent. Make sure to clarify what is included in the rent, and adjust your budget accordingly.

Subsidized Housing is run by the government and non-profit organizations and provides affordable housing for seniors, persons with disabilities and families with children.

The Credit Check

Most landlords in Canada will use a credit check to assess your credit worthiness. Since you are a newcomer to Canada, you may be asked to provide other verification to ensure that you can pay the rent. You may also be asked to provide references from previous landlords.

If you are a first-time renter, have had credit problems or do not have a credit rating, you may also need a guarantor's letter from a parent or close friend stating that the guarantor will assume the risk if the you fail to pay the rent.

In Canada there are two credit bureaus; Equifax and Trans Union. As you settle in your new country and start building a credit, you can check your credit rating yourself.
When you make loan, bill payments and the minimum credit card payment on time, you will get a good credit rating as it shows that you are responsible with regard to finances and that you can handle credit well. If you miss or make late payments several times, your credit rating will suffer.

Links:

- Classifieds: links to major daily papers in Canada, where you can find rental listings. Most coffee shops and libraries also let you read newspapers for free - http://www.w3newspapers.com/canada/

- Yellowpages.ca: Rentals can be found in the Apartment section

- www.craigslist.org

- www.kijiji.ca

- Rentboard: https://www.rentboard.ca/rentals/

- www.rentershotline.com

- www.prop2go.com

- www.housingblock.com

- Average cost of housing for immigrants:http://www.cic.gc.ca/english/resources/research/housing/cost.asp

13. Buying a house

The housing affordability in Canada varies greatly, with relatively high cost in the largest cities - especially Vancouver and Toronto – and more stable and affordable cost of home ownership in other parts of the country. Before you buy a home in Canada there are many factors to consider. I will cover some of them in this chapter.

If you decide to buy a house in Canada, it is important to remember that it is common to have a negotiation where the buyer gives one offer, the seller a counter-offer, the buy a counter-offer…you get the picture. This is not unusual, but do NOT enter into a win-at-all-cost war. You must set yourself some limits.

Budget

Remember that as an immigrant you probably won`t be eligible for a mortgage from your present bank in your home country, and since you haven`t managed to build a credit history in Canada it is very difficult to get a mortgage immediately. If you don`t have enough capital (from e.g. sale of your current assets) you may have to wait until you have built a credit history in Canada to buy a property.

Some exceptions apply, e.g. if your bank has a branch in Canada. Some banks in Canada have special services intended for newcomers, e.g. Bank of Montreal ("Newstart" program, see link below). Most banks require however that you have a permanent resident status to be eligible for a credit card or other loans.

The debt-to-income ratio (DTI) can help you calculate how much money you can loan. The DTI is your fixed monthly expenses divided by your gross monthly income. A healthy DTI is estimated at 10 to 20 or even 30 percent.

Costs related to the closing of a property sale

- Property tax. The property tax credit – already paid by the previous owners – you will have to cover. I paid approximately 220 $ when I bought my house in property tax. This is a tax you must pay yearly, usually in three installments. I pay approximately 550 $ in property tax as I paid a very low price for my house. More expensive properties will have a much higher property tax as this tax is relative to the value of the property.

- Legal fees and government related charges. I paid approximately 700 $ in legal fees and 570 $ in government related charges when I bought my house. These fees and charges will probably vary a great deal depending on the province and area where you want to buy a property.

- Mortgage fees. The mortgage fees vary depending on the size of the mortgage and other factors.

- Home inspection: A home inspection is a non-invasive inspection of the house done by a certified home inspector. It is often done when a property is sold, [...] the state of the house. Usually the buyer pays for the home inspection [...] e wants to have a home inspection done (I advise all buyers to have [...] ve, a home inspection cost approximately 500 $.

Certified Home Inspector in Whistler

Taxes and home insurance

Provincial and municipal property tax, waste and sewer management fees will vary depending on where you live. I pay approximately 600 $ per year.

Home insurance costs vary across Canada, with average yearly premiums of 700-900 $ depending on location and value of property.

The prices are rough average prices just meant as an indicator of the price level in the region. The rental prices are indicators of renting a 3-bedroom apartment in the provincial capitals in each province.

Property Prices

Whether you should buy a house or rent depends on many factors, some of which are:

- How long do you plan to live in this place?
- How stable is your income?
- Do you have enough money for a down payment? 5 % down payment is usually required in Canada (10 % if you are self-employed)
- Do you have enough money for the closing costs?
- How heavy is your total debt burden? It should not be more than 30-36 % of your gross income.
- Are you mentally ready to buy a house?
- Do you have enough money for maintenance and property taxes?

Below I have included a table summarizing the approximate average rental and property prices in Canada.

Table 1. Rent and house prices in the different provinces

Province	House price	Rent 3 bedroom apt	
		In city center	Outside city center
Alberta	400 000	2000	1500
British Columbia	600 000	3000	2000
Manitoba	250 000	1500	1300
New Brunswick	160 000	1100	900
Newfoundland and Labrador	300 000	1800	1200
Northwest Territories	400 000	2600	2700
Nova Scotia	250 000	1800	1200
Ontario	460 000	2600	1700
Prince Edward Island	150 000	1000	800
Saskatchewan	280 000	1700	1500
Quebec	280 000	1200	900
Yukon	350 000	1800	1400
Canada	430 000	1800	1400

I am not giving any advice, except that as with any big decisions it is smart to use some time to consider all the factors.

Links

- The Canadian Real Estate Association: http://crea.ca/content/national-average-price-map
- RBC Canadian Housing Forecast: http://www.rbc.com/economics/economic-reports/canadian-housing-forecast.html
- Government of Canada Immigration and Citizenship: http://www.cic.gc.ca/english/newcomers/after-housing.asp

- Buying the First Home in Canada – What Newcomers Need to Know
  http://www.cmhc-schl.gc.ca/odpub/pdf/66144.pdf
- Real estate listing in Canada
  www.realtor.ca
- Canadian Real Estate Association
  www.crea.ca
- Point2Homes Canada real estate listings
  http://www.point2homes.com/CA
- Remax real estate listings
  www.remax.ca
- Canadian Real Estate Magazine
  http://www.canadianrealestatemagazine.ca/
- Royal LePage real estate listings
  http://www.royallepage.ca/
- Century 21 real estate listings
  http://www.century21.ca/
- Canada Housing and Mortgage Corporation
  http://www.cmhc-schl.gc.ca/en/co/buho/
- Mortgages Canada
  http://www.mortgagescanada.ca/mortgages/mortgage-down-payment/
- Bidding war basics for buyers
  http://www.hgtv.ca/realestate/article/bidding-war-basics-for-buyers/

14. Banks and Credit Unions

Canada has two different kind of financial institution. There are the traditional banks, which are for profit private financial corporation. Canada's banks are regulated by the federal government and regulated pursuant to the *Bank Act.* Then there are the credit unions, which have a reputation of being community oriented. They are owned by their members, and regulated by the provincial government. The credit unions are not for profit, and they are typically created for a particular reason, e.g. to serve members based on geography.

Many of the large banks in Canada have programs specifically developed for newcomers, and below you can find links to some of these programs. Usually you won`t be able to loan money or get a credit card in Canada until you are a permanent resident or citizen. As long as you have a time-limited work permit, you will only be able to have a debit card. One solution is to have a credit card with a pre-payed amount you can use, e.g. you have a Visa card with a 1000 $ balance, and the balance must newer drop below a certain amount (e.g. 30 $). This can seem pointless as it will function in the same way as a debit card, but a very important reason is it helps you to build a credit rating in Canada.

I have an account in RBC Royal Bank, but plan to move my banking to Bank of Montreal later because they have a great Air Miles program.

Overview of Canadian banks and credit union:
https://en.wikipedia.org/wiki/List_of_banks_and_credit_unions_in_Canada

15. Cost of Living

The cost of living in Canada is lower compared to some European countries, while higher compared to some areas of the USA, Middle East, Africa, Asia and Europe. When you plan your move you should keep in mind that you will need money to cover the expenses of immigration processing fees and the transition period and it is smart to remember that we usually underestimate future costs so add some buffer.

Some consumer prices in Canada

The prices listed here are approximate prices, and all the expenses and prices are just examples from one area of Canada. Depending on where you live in Canada, the prices can be lower or higher. These examples are just to give you an idea about what price level you can expect in Canada.

Dining out
- Meal, Inexpensive Restaurant 12 $
- McMeal at McDonalds 7 $

Dairy

- Milk (regular), (2 liter) 3.69 $
- Yoghurt (650 g) 4.29 $
- Eggs (12) 2.50 $
- Whipped topping, spray can 2.89 $
- Local Cheese (1kg) 8.80 $

Meats

- Chicken Breasts (Boneless, Skinless), (1kg) 8.80 $
- Beef Round (1kg) 11.50 $

Produce

- Apples (1kg) 2.80 $
- Banana (1kg) 1.96 $
- Coleslaw (274 g) 1.69 $
- Mushrooms Cremini (227 g) 2.79 $
- Mushrooms Portobello (400 g)5.49.$
- Baby carrots (907 g) 3.49 $
- Sweet onion (453 g) 2.49 $
- White onion (453 g) 2.49 $

Groceries

- Tikka Masala cooking sauce (650 ml) 2.49 $
- Soya (650 ml) 2.49 $
- Pasta sauce (jar) 1.69 $
- Penne 2.39 $

Grooming

- Vidal Sassoon 750 ml shampoo 5.99 $
- Nivea deodorant 2.49 $
- L'Oréal studio line hair gel 8.49 $
- Physician formula face powder, mineral 16.99 $
- Nice'n Easy hair color 12.49 $

Utilities (Monthly)

- Basic (Electricity, Heating, Water, Garbage) for 75m2 Apartment 110 $

Cell phone subscription and Internet

- Moto X Play cell phone (0 $) with 1 year subscription (unlimited local calling, unlimited texting and 500 MB shareable data 50 $/month
- In rural area (100 Mbps download, 10 Mbps upload, 250 GB bandwidth monthly usage, fiber optic network) 97.95 $/month

Transportation
- Monthly Pass (Regular Price) 70 $
- Gasoline (1 liter) $ 0.99
- 2013 Dodge Journey SUV 2.4L 4-cyl. 4-speed Automatic 11.500 $

Clothes and shoes
- GAP Sweater 55 $
- GAP pants 69$
- Nike athletic shoes 65$
- Sweater (inexpensive brand) 20-30 $

Table 2. Example of a household budget in Canada

Budget post	Per year
Income (after taxes)	49392
Mortgage	7760
Car loan	6040
Food expenditures	4800
Insurance	1860
Oil	1200
Electricity	984
Cell phone	1020
Internet	1152
Property tax, savage	324
Car maintenance	240
Transportation (gas)	1440
Health care	960
Personal grooming	960
Sports	960
Clothes, shoes	960
Recreation (music, TV & film streaming etc.)	960
Misc. debt	3400
Home maintenance	336

16 Utility providers

When you are choosing a utility provider, I suggest asking neighbors in the area where you live for advice.

Locals usually know the best companies that service the area, and you may get some useful tips. Below I have listed a few examples, but there are many more providers in addition to the ones listed below. Check out the links at the end of the chapter to find more information about utility providers.

Electricity service providers:

- British Columbia — BC Hydro
- Ontario — several options, including Hydro One and Toronto Hydro
- Alberta — Energy Alberta
- Saskatchewan — SaskPower
- Manitoba — Manitoba Hydro
- Quebec — Hydro Quebec
- PEI — Maritime Electric
- New Brunswick — NB Power
- Nova Scotia — Nova Scotia Power
- Newfoundland — Newfoundland & Labrador Hydro

Heating Oil Service Provider

The winters in Canada can be cold, so make sure you are prepared well in advance. Many houses in Canada use oil for heating. Here is a list of some companies that deliver oil for heating:

- Petro Canada
- Shell Canada
- Irving
- The Energy Co-Op

Links:
Heating oil suppliers
- Shell: http://www.shell.ca/en/products-services/in-the-home.html
- Petro Canada: http://www.petro-canada.ca/en/homeheating/3231.aspx
- Irving Energy: https://www.irvingenergy.com/heating-oil-propane/delivery/
- Coop Energy: https://www.theenergy.coop/heating-oil

Electric utilities
- Utility rate comparisons
  https://www.hydro.mb.ca/regulatory_affairs/energy_rates/electricity/utility_rate_comp.shtml
- List of electricity
  https://en.wikipedia.org/wiki/List_of_Canadian_electric_utilities

NOTE!

Some water heaters in Canadian homes use oils as energy source, so even in the summer you may need to make sure your oil tank is filled

17. Phone and Internet providers

Which provider you choose as your cell phone and internet provider depends on where you live. Some providers deliver the best internet service in some rural areas while other providers are better in other areas. The same is true for cell phones. In the area where I live – which is quite rural – Eastlink delivers a very good broadband, while Bell is a good choice for cell phones.

I recommend asking neighbors, colleagues and other people who live in the area where you live for the best providers in that area as this can vary greatly according to where you live.

Cell phones and cell phone services

1. Bell delivers TV, internet and cell phone services across Canada and you can read more at www.bell.ca.
2. Another provider of the same services – TV, internet, home phone and home security – is Rogers. I am not familiar with this provider, but Rogers is one of the largest providers of cable TV in Ontario, New Brunswick and Newfoundland and Labrador. You can read more about Rogers at www.rogers.com.
3. Telus Mobility is another provider of cell phone services. You can read more at www.telus.com.

Internet and TV

The same companies that provide cell phone services, also provide internet and TV services.

1. Eastlink provides internet, TV, home phones and home security services. You can read more at www.eastlink.ca
2. Bell provides internet and TV services. In the area where I live, Eastlink is the best and most stable internet provider, and in other areas Bell or Rogers may provide the best service. Again I advise you

to ask neighbors and the locals to find out which company provide the best service in the area where you live. Internet service can vary greatly depending on where you live in Canada.

3. Rogers – www.rogers.com

Another thing to keep in mind is that you must provide valid documentation of Canadian residency before you can subscribe to any services. You must provide e.g. a driver's license (or other valid photo identification) and you may need a social insurance number. Until you get a permanent resident card you may also have to pay in advance for any services.

18. Transportation

The large cities in Canada enjoy great public transportation. Buses, skytrains and trams provide regular transit times within the large cities and for those who live in rural areas buying a car is probably a smart idea. Carpooling is also a possibility for those who live in the urban areas. If you are a student, you can buy an uPass which gives you unlimited access to public transportation on a monthly basis.

Since Canada is a large country with long distances the price for airline tickets between the different provinces can cost 400-700 $.

Greyhound is a great option if you have the time but wants to save some money. Greyhound buses connect North American cities, and give you the opportunity to see some of the country.

Driver`s license

To drive a car in Canada you need a driver`s license valid in the province you live in. Provincial and territorial governments issue driver`s licenses in Canada. If you have a valid license from your home country, you may be able to drive with this license for a short period. You should get an International Driving Permit (IDP) in your home country before you leave. The requirements for you to obtain a valid driver`s license in the province you want to live in depends on the provincial laws and from which country you move.

When I arrived on Prince Edward Island, I were permitted to drive with my Norwegian driver`s license for up to 4 months after arrival. The provincial government here has a list of countries and if your home country is on this list you may only be required to change your current driver`s license into a provincial one without having to pass any tests. I was not so lucky so I had to do a written test first on the "Rules of The

Road" (see link to relevant province). When I passed the written test I had to pass a driver`s test. I passed both on first trials, and I admit it was useful to do the tests since quite a few of the rules are different from my home country. The cost for both tests was less then CAD 100, so it is not a major expense.

To drive a car in Canada you need a valid car insurance (it is illegal to drive without one). Remember to bring documents to verify driving and insurance history from your home country. In Norway I got these documents from the police (a police certificate) and from my insurance company. The insurance company should verify how many years you had a car insured in your home country, how many claims you have had and details pertaining to the claims (date, incident, insurance claim). Be aware that the cost of your insurance may be high if you have had any claims and if you don`t have a "clean" driving history.

Once you get your insurance documents in order you can register your car with the provincial government (see links below). To register a vehicle you need:

- •Current vehicle registration papers (if you brought a car from your home country);
- •Valid pink liability insurance card
- •Valid credit card. Visa or MasterCard are accepted most places.

For general information: http://www.cic.gc.ca/english/newcomers/after-transportation-driving.asp

Buying a car

Apart from your budget and obvious requirements, newcomers should also consider what kind of purpose their car will serve. If you're keen to take advantage of the majestic Canadian mountains and national parks, you may want to consider buying a four wheel drive; whereas if you're mostly going to use your car for city driving in Vancouver or Toronto, then something compact is a smart choice.

Buying a car from a dealership gives you the advantage of buying the car with warranties. Car dealers usually also help you with taking care of the paperwork, like registration and insurance. As in all countries, be aware of the usual smooth-talking salesmen. A healthy dose of critical thinking and skepticism protect you from paying too much or buying a car you`ll later regret.

Buying a used car from a private seller

You can save a few thousand dollars if you buy a used car from a private seller. I bought my used car from a private seller, and I probably saved approximately 2000 $. I have had no major problems. I recommend however that you have the car examined by a mechanic before you buy it.

Canada has a lot of great web pages which can help you in comparing the cost of vehicles and researching reasonable price compared to amenities, mileage and accessories.

If buying privately, you'll be responsible for getting insurance coverage and registration the car. The seller has to fill out forms that make the transfer of car ownership official.

Links:

- www.autonet.ca
- www.auto123

- www.autotrader.ca
- www.autos.ca
- www.MonsterAuto.ca

19. Insurance

Buying insurance as a newcomer in Canada can be expensive, but to make sure that you get the best possible price it is smart to get quotes from different insurance providers before you decide. I saved approximately 500 $ per year by getting quotes from two different insurance companies, so the extra time you spend is well worth the effort.

Car insurance

If you are going to buy car insurance, it is also important to bring these documents with you:

- Driving history report (also called drivers abstract). This can be obtained from the issuer of driver's licenses in your home country, or from the police.
- Vehicle claims history (from your insurance company)

The insurance price depends on:

- ✓ Your driving history
- ✓ Your claims history
- ✓ the safety features and statistics of your vehicle
- ✓ the year, make and model of your vehicle
- ✓ Where you live
- ✓ What kind of insurance you want

- ✓ For how many years you have had a driver's license
- ✓ How many persons are going to use the car
- ✓ If you commute to work and how much you'll use the car
- ✓ Crime and claims statistics for your neighborhood
- ✓

Car insurance price varies greatly depending on where you live in Canada, with Ontario being the most expensive and Prince Edward Island and Quebec being the cheapest. I live on Prince Edward Island, but as a newcomer I pay well above the average car insurance so my annual premium is approximately CAD 1400. I have a clean driving history and I have one previous claim (no fault claim) during my approximately 10 year driving history. I got quotes from two different insurance companies, The Co-operators and an insurance broker, and the broker cost approximately CAD 500 more in annual premium.

Some Insurance Companies in Canada

Here is a list of some insurance companies in Canada (note that this list is not a recommendation, but merely some of your options):

- CAA is a federation of 9 automotive clubs serving about 5 million members through 130 offices across Canada. CAA provides a wide range of member services and products to improve travelling and motoring conditions at home and around the world. Some of the insurance products they offer include auto insurance for your car which is available to you by telephone and Internet. Read more at http://www.caa.ca/

- Aviva Canada is one of the leading Property and Casualty insurance groups in Canada, providing home, automobile and business insurance and premier claims service to more than 3 million customers. Read more at http://www.aviva.com/#about

- BMO Insurance Part of BMO Financial Group. BMO Insurance provide life -, travel- and accident and illness insurance. Read more at https://www.bmo.com/insurance/life-insurance?ecid=ps-INSSEME001INS2-SADAD45&adid=WGOCNLI*1**E#

- CAA Health & Dental Insurance provide health, dental and life insurance. Read more at http://www.caahealth.ca/?assocId=CAAMT&province=PE&webPlanId=000131

- The Co-operators: The Co-operators Group Limited (CGL) is a Canadian-owned co-operative with over 65 years of history and with more than 2 million customers. If you buy a Coop membership at a Coop grocery store close to where you live you will get a small discount on the billing, and if you buy both home and car insurance you get 10-15 % discount. There are also other group benefits, and this is the insurance company where I have my car insurance. They provide excellent service, great insurance and member benefits and don`t overprice the premium because you are a newcomer. Read more at http://www.cooperatorsgroupinsurance.ca/

- Economical Insurance is one of the largest property and casualty insuranc companies in Canada, providing home, automobile and commercial insurance products to over one million policyholders across Canada. Read more at http://www.economicalinsurance.com/en/

- Empire Life The Empire Life Insurance Company (Empire Life) offers a full range of financial products and services - including personal life insurance, critical illness coverage, investment options, group life and health benefits and group RSP plans. Head Office is located in Kingston, Ontario, Canada.

- Equitable Life of Canada provide life and critical illness insurance in addition to various group benefit insurances. Read more at http://www.equitable.ca/en/

- Federated Insurance Company of Canada is a niche insurer specializing in property and casualty insurance for several commercial markets, for example contractors, auto dealers, equipment dealers, restaurants, grocery stores, woodworking, home builders', electricians, plumbers, heating and air conditioning, manufacturing, retail and wholesale,life and group benefits. Read more at http://www.federated.ca/

- Intact Financial is Canada's largest provider of home, auto, and business insurance.

- Manulife Financial (Manufacturers Life Insurance Company) is a major Canadian insurance company and financial services provider.

- RBC Insurance® provides a wide range of travel, life, health, home, auto, wealth and reinsurance products and solutions, as well as creditor and business insurance services, to individual, business and group clients. Read more at: http://www.rbcinsurance.com/supportcentre/clientsupport/about_us.html

Home Insurance

Aviva, Co-Operators, Federated Insurance, Intact Financial and Industrial Alliance are some of the top Canadian home insurance companies. I recommend also in this instance that you ask for quotes from two or three different companies to get the best insurance for your needs. Usually the company will send an insurance agent to your home for a home appraisal before you can get a quote. The annual premium will vary greatly depending on the value, age and state of your home as well as where it is located.

20. Some success stories

I have included the stories about some immigrants I know in the hope that these stories will inspire you and encourage to begin a challenging yet amazing journey to Canada. Often the stories and tales that are repeated and told time and again are often the extremely tragic or the extremely successful stories. The stories below are neither, as they are the true stories of some very "average" immigrants who have managed to succeed in Canada because of patience, persistence and resourcefulness. I have changed the names and some other details to protect the privacy of these common but yet unique stories.

Anna from Sweden

Anna from Sweden received a job offer in Canada as a Quality Assurance Manager at the end of April 2015. She traveled to Canada one month later to prepare for the move. She bought a small house in a small, coastal community and a few weeks later she bought a car. Anna received a provincial nomination from the province in which she settled.

When she received the nomination, she drove to the USA, and as she returned and reentered Canada at the Houlton border she was granted a work permit lasting 3 years. The work permit allows her to only to work for her current employer, and for the maximum time allowed for in the work permit (3 years). She cannot study in Canada. She can obtain a social security number (valid for the same period) and she can obtain health care benefits (e.g. she can apply for a Health card). Although the process entailed a lot of paperwork and a lot of work during the first few months, Anna is now thriving in her new job. It took 2 months and 9 days from Anna received her job offer until she started in her job and had settled down. After she received her work permit, she sent an application for a permanent resident card.

The permanent residency processing takes a bit longer, but already 3 months after she sent the application, she received a request for a medical examination and another few months later she received a permanent residency in Canada. She can now work and study anywhere in Canada. She is also protected under Canadian law and the *Canadian Charter of Rights and Freedoms* and she receives most social benefits that Canadian citizens receive, including health care coverage. She is still a Swedish citizen, so she cannot vote in Canada, but that is basically the only restriction.

Every week she hikes along the beautiful beaches where she lives, and she enjoys the friendliness of the Canadians and the vast opportunities her new home country has to offer her.

Below is a timeline indicating Anna`s journey toward Canadian citizenship. This is a route you also can take.

Asaf from Algeria

Asaf is an engineer, who moved to Spain to obtain a PhD. While in Spain he applied for and received a Canadian permanent residency. When he finished his PhD he got a post doc position in Canada, and moved to Canada together with his fiancé. Now, 5 years later, he recently obtained his Canadian citizenship. He and his fiancé are happy in Canada, and he enjoys the freedom and tolerance of the Canadian people. He moved to Canada in the autumn, so he advices immigrants from warmer climates to be prepared for the winter. As a newcomer the climate change can be tough, but now Asaf loves the winter and all the possibilities for winter sport activities it has to offer.

Erico from Brazil

Erico is an intellectual introvert from Sao Paulo who loves Canada because of the vast space and the possibility to be himself – an introvert. He has a PhD in genomics and a career in biotech is a smart choice in Canada due to the nations large and diverse biotech industry.

Erico thrives in Canada and has recently become a dad for the first time to a beautiful baby boy. He met his fiancé in Canada, and his story is a true romantic tale.

And so can your story be if you are dedicated, resourceful and open to all the possibilities Canada has to offer.

21. Appendix

1. Relocation check list

Three to six months before your move

- Renew passport if necessary
- Begin your work permit (or other immigration track) application process.
- Assess your language skills and start a language course if necessary. Take an IELTS language test if required for your work permit
- Check baggage and customs limitations.
- Buy travel and health insurance
- Arrange accommodation in Canada
- Arrange your banking—Visa/Master card can be used anywhere in Canada, but it is smart to carry a small amount of cash in addition

Two-Three months before you move

- If you have children, notify any schools and arrange for school records to be transferred to the new school.
- Decide what you will bring with you and what you will leave behind – create an inventory:
  - Two (2) copies of a detailed list of all the personal or household items you are bringing with you

- - Two (2) copies of a list of items that are arriving later and their money value
  - use the Canada Border Services Agency`s Personal Effects Accounting Document
- Get estimates from international moving companies for moving and/or check out options for storage of your furniture and belongings. Make arrangements.
- Purchase equipment to assist in your move including removals boxes, labels, tape, bubble wrap, marker pens and plenty of newspaper (for wrapping china etc.).
- Check to see if you need any permits for the move with Canada Border Services Agency – www.cbsa.gc.ca

Four-Seven weeks before the move

- Notify important service providers (phone company, bank, postal service etc.) about your new address
- Notify authorities of your move (if applicable)
- Take care of any health issues, make sure you have prescription medicines for 3 months
- Make arrangements for importation of pets, vehicle and other important items

Three-Four weeks before the move

- Confirm your personal travel arrangements
- Arrange transportation to/from the airport at home and in Canada.
- Research telephone, internet, TV and utilities providers in your new location
- Check out insurance coverage during move
- Cancel insurance, internet TV and phone subscriptions

Two weeks before the move

- Clean empty cupboards and drawers - it's good to treat others as you would want to be treated.
- Arrange for disposal of large items
- If you are driving, ensure your car has recently been serviced.
- Cancel newspaper and magazine deliveries
- Notify credit cards, loan companies etc. of your change of address

One week before the move

- Empty the freezer and start to finish food in the fridge
- Check that all the light bulbs work and replace any non-functioning lightbulbs.
- Clean the empty cupboards

One day before the move

- Defrost the freezer and fridge - make sure that the door is left open.
- Disconnect washing machines etc. and prepare for the move
- Pack a box of things that will be needed the first few days
- Check what time your moving company will arrive the next day.
- Charge your mobile phone.

- Make sure you have access to money in the correct currency when you arrive at your destination

Removal Day

- Read all meters (gas, electric, water) and make a note of the readings (if you have a camera you might want to take photo's as evidence)
- Lock all windows and doors
- Oversee all the unloading and unpacking – check for damages
- If possible, read the meters (gas, electric, water)
- Ensure all of your documents are in order and make photocopies to pack in your baggage, to leave at home, and to send to your email address. These documents include:
  - Passport
  - Airline tickets
  - Travel insurance certificate
  - Letter of acceptance for your Canadian educational institution or job contract
  (if applicable)

  - Key addresses and phone numbers
  - A bank statement showing proof of funds
  - Letter of introduction from Canadian immigration, if applicable
  - Prescriptions for any medication you are carrying
  - Traveler's cheques, if applicable
  - Medical and immunization records
  - Academic history and university transcripts
  - Other valuable items such as prescription medication (be sure to get enough to last you a few months), bank cards, cash, keys, emergency phone numbers, specific personal hygiene products and so on. It's very important that all the above-mentioned valuables stay with you at all times during the preparation and the actual relocation overseas.

2. Useful web pages

Immigration, Government of Canada web pages

- government of Canada, Immigration and citizenship: This is the web page you should primarily use, and you will find most of the information you need for your immigration process at this web page
  http://www.cic.gc.ca/english/index.asp

- Government of Canada, Service Canada, Immigration and Newcomers: You will find some useful information about housing, health, income and legal assistant, personal documents and much more
  http://www.servicecanada.gc.ca

- Visa offices outside of Canada
  http://www.cic.gc.ca/english/information/offices/apply-where.asp

- Where can you get a police check? List of all countries
  http://www.cic.gc.ca/english/infORmation/security/police-cert/index.asp

Immigration, Provincial or Territorial Government web pages

- Government of Alberta, Immigration Programs & Services
  http://www.albertacanada.com/opportunity.aspx

- Government of Ontario, Immigration Programs & Services
  http://www.ontarioimmigration.ca/en/

- Government of Quebec, Immigration Programs & Services
  http://www.immigration-quebec.gouv.qc.ca/en/

- Government of Saskatchewan, Immigration Programs & Services
  http://www.economy.gov.sk.ca/immigration

- Government of Newfoundland and Labrador, Immigration Programs & Services
  http://www.nlimmigration.ca/

- Government of Yukon, Immigration Programs & Services
  http://www.education.gov.yk.ca/Immigration.html

- Northwest Territories Immigration Portal
  http://www.immigratenwt.ca/

Immigration, Provincial or Territorial Nominee programs

- Ontario PNP:
  http://www.ontarioimmigration.ca/en/pnp/index.htm

- British Columbia PNP:
  http://www.welcomebc.ca/Immigrate/About-the-BC-PNP.aspx

- Alberta PNP:
  http://albertacanada.com/opportunity/immigrating/ainp.aspx

- Newfoundland and Labrador PNP:
  http://www.nlpnp.ca/index.html

- Saskatchewan Immigrant Nominee Program (SINP):
  http://www.economy.gov.sk.ca/immigration/sinp

- Manitoba PNP:
  http://www.immigratemanitoba.com/immigrate/

- New Brunswick PNP:
  http://www.welcomenb.ca/content/wel-
  bien/en/immigrating_and_settling/how_to_immigrate/new_brunswick_provincialnomineeprogram
  .html

- Yukon PNP:
  http://www.education.gov.yk.ca/YNP.html

- Prince Edward Island PNP:
  http://www.gov.pe.ca/immigration/index.php3?number=1014385

- Northwest Territories Nominee Program (NTNP):
  http://www.immigratenwt.ca/en/nwt-nominee-program

Private immigration sites

- http://www.immigration.ca/en/

- http://www.canadavisa.com/

- http://canadianimmigrant.ca/

- The Immigration Canada Fair connects Newcomers, Temporary Foreign Workers, landed Immigrants and International Students with providers of employment, education & training, foreign credential, entrepreneurship, immigration and settlement services across Canada http://www.immigrationcanadafair.com/

- Migrationexpert – a private immigration company with a team of highly experienced ICCRC regulated migration consultants https://www.migrationexpert.ca/visa_canada/

Automobiles

AutoPartsWey.ca - Wholesale auto parts and accessories

eBay Canada, motor – Online sale of vehicles, auto parts, accessories, tools and supplies and much more

CarcostCanada – Online web page with information about car pricing. Great page if you want to negotiate price

Canadian Tire – Auto parts and accessories

Insurance Hotline – Web page that give quotes from different insurance companies

Kenatix – Compare quotes from different insurance companies

Home and hardware

https://www.theshoppingchannel.com

https://www.homedepot.ca

http://www.sears.ca/

http://www.walmart.ca/en

http://www.thebay.com

http://www.cymax.ca

https://www.lowes.ca

https://www.jysk.ca/

Public transit

Ottawa – http://www.octranspo1.com/splash

Halifax – http://www.halifax.ca/metrotransit/

Calgary – www.calgarytransit.com

Edmonton – http://www.edmonton.ca/transportation/edmonton-transit-system-ets.aspx

Montreal – http://www.stm.info/english/a-somm.htm

Toronto – www.ttc.ca

Vancouver – www.translink.ca

3. Metric to Standard Conversion

1 gram = 0.035ounces

1 kilogram = 2.20 pounds

1 kilogram = 35.27 ounces

1 tonnes = 1.10 ton, short

1 milliliter = 0.033814 fluid ounces

1 liter= 33.814022 fluid ounces

1 liter= 2.113376 pints

1 kiloliter= 264.1721 gallons

1 inch = 2.54 cm

1 foot = 30.48 cm

1 yard = 91.44 cm

1 mile = 1609 m

Links:

Metric to Standard http://www.worldwidemetric.com/Measurements.html

4. Canada facts
- Capital: Ottawa
- Largest city: Toronto
- Official languages: English and French
- Currency: Canadian dollar ($) (CAD)
- Government:
- Federal parliamentary;
  - o   Prime Minister Justin Trudeau
  - o   constitutional monarchy; Monarch Elizabeth II
- Population: Approximately 35,985,751
- Ethnic groups:
  76.7% White
  14.2% Asian
  4.3% Aboriginal
  2.9% Black
  1.2% Latin American
  0.5% multiracial
  0.3% other

What's important to Canadians? Ice hockey, Tim Hortons, yellow school buses and staying warm in the winter

I wish you a happy journey to your

new home, Canada

The End

46038837R00044

Made in the USA
San Bernardino, CA
23 February 2017